THE COMPLETE TRADITIONAL WEDDING ALBUM

for Organ, Keyboard, and Voice

Selected and Edited by
ROLLIN SMITH

DOVER PUBLICATIONS, INC.
Mineola, New York

Bibliographical Note

This Dover edition, first published in 2005, is a new collection. Some works are
reprinted from early editions, while others have been arranged specially for this volume.

International Standard Book Number

ISBN-13: 978-0-486-43963-1
ISBN-10: 0-486-43963-1

Manufactured in the United States by Courier Corporation
4500058496
www.doverpublications.com

INTRODUCTION

THIS COLLECTION includes the most frequently requested traditional music for weddings, as well as additional works suitable for the occasion. With this book you may be confident that you will be able to provide music for any ceremony, from the simplest to the most urbane. The volume is arranged in three sections: organ music for the prelude, as the guests are being seated, and organ/piano/keyboard music for the processional and recessional. Vocal solos as well as eight hymns provide singers with a varied selection from which to choose. Many weddings have program booklets for the guests so it is possible to reproduce the hymns in this volume to be sung by those attending the service.

Much of the music is technically easy. Considering the number of keyboards in churches, a generous selection of music for manuals only is included. Versions of more popular works are provided in alternate settings that will prove useful and flexible under varied circumstances.

It is common to have two processionals: one for the wedding party, which accompanies as many as twenty people down the aisle, and the *Bridal Chorus* from Wagner's *Lohengrin* reserved for the bride. Generally the processional is more dignified and stately while the recessional reflects the excitement and exhilaration of the ceremony's conclusion. There is no rule, however, so the music is grouped into one section and the bridal couple is free to choose any selection for either part of the service.

In addition to the music in this volume selections from Dover's many other collections are recommended: Widor's popular *Toccata* and Vierne's *Carillon de Westminster,* for instance, are both to be found in *Organ Classics.* Many works suitable for preludial music can be found in Dover's series of collections for manuals only.

Rollin Smith

CONTENTS

MUSIC FOR THE PRELUDE

PROCESSIONALS

VOCAL MUSIC

WEDDING HYMNS

MUSIC FOR THE PRELUDE

ARIA

"When Thou Art Near"

Swell = Vox Humana, St. Diap. & Open Diap. 8'
Choir (or Great) = Soft 8'
Pedal = Bourdon 16'
Coupler = Choir to Ped.

JOHANN SEBASTIAN BACH
1685–1750

Arranged by Clarence Eddy

YE SWEET RETREAT

Tell me, lovely Shepherd, where
Thou feed'st at noon thy fleecy lare.
Direct me to the Sweet Retreat
That guards thee from the Midday Heat.

Lest by the Flocks I lonely stray
Without a Guide and lose my Way.
Where rest at Noon thy bleating lare?
Gentle Shepherd, tell me where.

Transcribed by Rollin Smith

WILLIAM BOYCE
1711–1779

CHANSON DE MATIN

Op. 15, No. 2

Arranged by A. Herbert Brewer

EDWARD ELGAR
1857–1934

Sw. to Ped.

Gt to Ped. add 16 ft

Sw. to Ped.

à Mr. Paul POPEL

ÉPITHALAME

from *Shylock,* Op. 57

I. 16' and 8' Solo
II. 8' Accompaniment
Ped. 16' 8', II - Pedal

Arranged by Rollin Smith

GABRIEL FAURÉ
1845–1924

à Mr. Paul POPEL

NOCTURNE

from *Shylock*, Op. 57

Arranged by Rollin Smith

GABRIEL FAURÉ
1845–1924

LIEBESTRÄUM

Notturno No. 3

Arranged by Harvey B. Gaul

FRANZ LISZT
1811–1886

Poco Allegro con affeto

poco cresc. ed agitato

Sw. strings and
soft Diap.
ten.

Ch. melodia or Flute d'amour

18

BÉNÉDICTION NUPTIALE

Op. 9

CAMILLE SAINT-SAËNS
1835–1921

Hautb: et Flûtes de 8 et 4 pieds.

Poco   a   poco crescendo.

Sempre crescendo.

f

f

Poco a poco Diminuendo.

Clavier de récit. Jeux de fonds
de 8 et 4 pieds (boite ouverte.)

Mezzo piano.

BENEDIZIONE NUZIALE

Andante per Organo, Op. 30

Performed at the Church of S. Maria degli Angeli in Rome, October 24, 1896,
for the wedding ceremony of their royal Highnesses the Prince of Naples and
the Princess Elena of Montenegro

GIOVANNI SGAMBATI
1841–1914

TRÄUME

"Dreams"

(*Wesendonck Lieder*, No. 5)

Transcribed by William C. Carl

RICHARD WAGNER
1813–1883

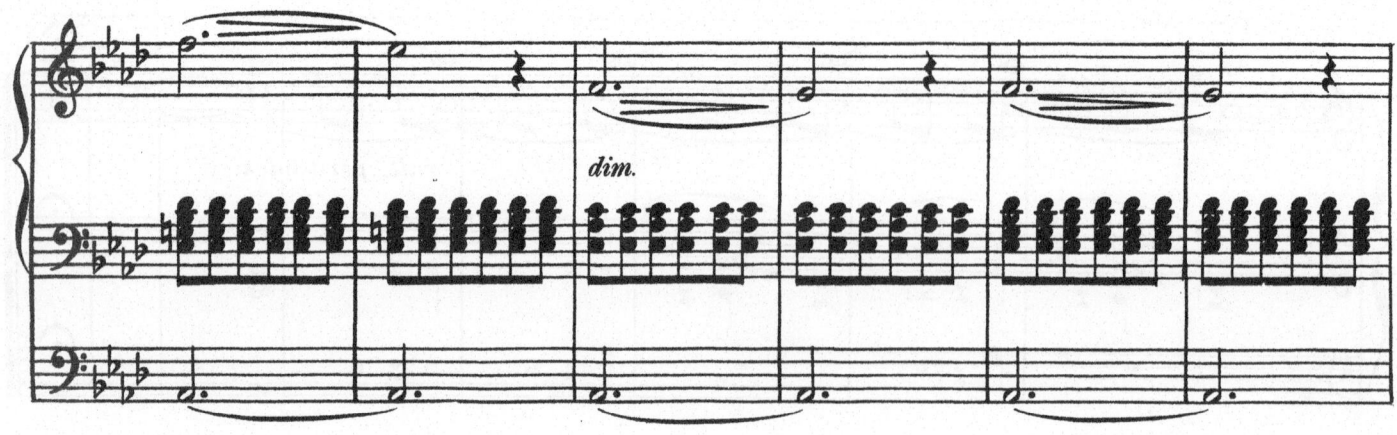

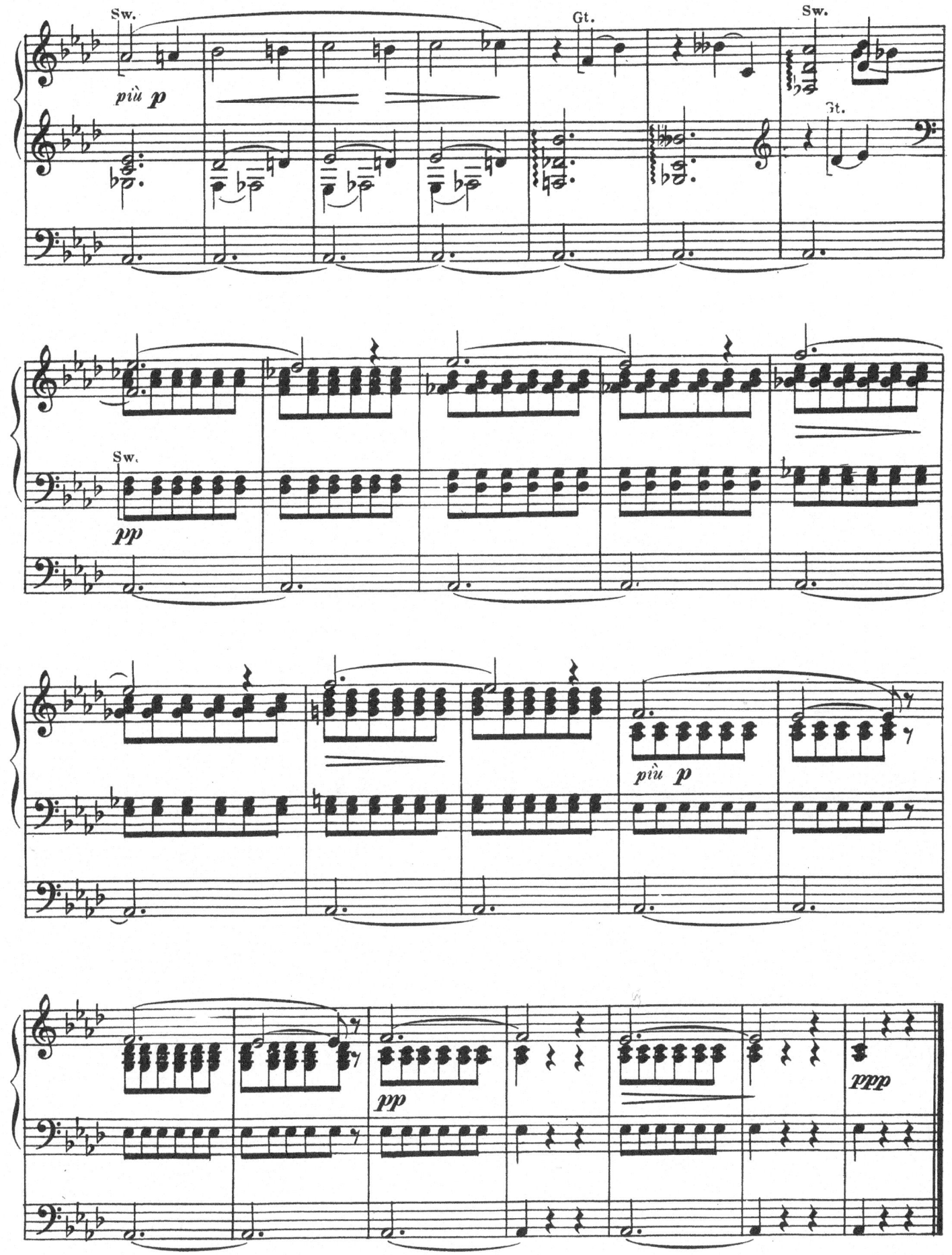

SÉRÉNADE

Transcribed by William J. Westbrook

CHARLES-MARIE WIDOR
1844–1937

ANGEL PROCESSION

from *La Vita Nuova*, Op. 9

Transcribed by Rollin Smith

ERMANNO WOLF-FERRARI
1876–1948

The instrumentation is for two harps and piano with timpani and strings playing the bass. Registration should duplicate the effect as closely as possible, i.e. Harp or Celesta 8' and 4' with clear 16' and 8' pedal stops.

PROCESSIONALS

TRUMPET TUNE

HENRY PURCELL
1659–1695

PRÉLUDE-RONDEAU

Prelude to the *Te Deum*

I. Trumpet
II. Principals 8' 4' 2'
Ped. 16' 8', I - Pedal

Arranged by Rollin Smith

MARC-ANTOINE CHARPENTIER
1645–1704

Maestoso

CANON IN D

Arranged by Rollin Smith

JOHANN PACHELBEL
1653–1706

Andante sostenuto

RIGAUDON

from *Idoménée*

Full Swell
Great to 15th
Choir 8' 4'
Pedal: 16' & 8', Great to Pedal
Manuals coupled

Arranged by Gustave Ferrari

ANDRÉ CAMPRA
1660–1744

RONDEAU

from *Sinfonies des Fanfares,* Première Suite

I.   8' Trumpet
II.   Foundation stops 8' and 4'
III. Flutes 8' and 4'
Pedal 16' and 8'
      II - Pedal

JEAN-JOSEPH MOURET
1682–1738

Arranged by Rollin Smith

58

THE PRINCE OF DENMARK'S MARCH

from *A Choice Collection of Ayres for the Harpsichord or Spinett*

London, 1700

JEREMIAH CLARKE
1673–1707

TRUMPET VOLUNTARY

The Prince of Denmark's March

Arranged by Rollin Smith

JEREMIAH CLARKE
1673–1707

TRUMPET TUNE AND TRIO

JEREMIAH CLARKE
1673–1707

MARCHE

from *Les Fêtes d'Hébé*

II.   8' Trumpet
I.   8' and 4' foundation stops
III. Cornet (8' 4' 2⅔' 2' 1⅗')

JEAN-PHILIPPE RAMEAU
1683–1764

Arranged by Rollin Smith

AIR

from *The Water Music*

Arranged by Rollin Smith

GEORGE FRIDERIC HANDEL
1685–1759

ALLEGRO MÆSTOSO

"With Trumpets and Horns"

from *The Water Music*

Arranged by Rollin Smith

GEORGE FRIDERIC HANDEL
1685–1759

TRUMPET TUNE

from Voluntary I in D Major

WILLIAM BOYCE
1711–1779

TRUMPET TUNE

from Voluntary V, Op. 5, No. 5

I.   8' Trumpet
III. 8' Stopped Diapason, 4' Flute and/or 4' Principal

JOHN STANLEY
1713–1786

TRUMPET TUNE

from Voluntary V, Op. 6, No. 5

I.   8' Trumpet
II. Cornet V or 8' Hautboy
III. 8' Stopped Diapason, 4' Flute and/or 4' Principal

JOHN STANLEY
1713–1786

PSALM 19

THE HEAVENS DECLARE THE GLORY OF GOD

Transcribed by Théodore Dubois

BENEDETTO MARCELLO
1686–1739

Full Organ with Manuals Coupled (Swell closed)
Great and Choir coupled to Pedal

ODE TO JOY

Arranged by Rollin Smith

LUDWIG VAN BEETHOVEN
1770–1827

Mæstoso

fff

+ Solo Tuba to Pedal and 32'

BRIDAL CHORUS

from *Lohengrin*

Swell: 8' and 4' with Oboe
Great: 8' Gamba, Swell to Great
Choir: soft 8' and 4'
Pedal: 16' Bourdon, Swell to Pedal

Transcribed by Preston Ware Orem

RICHARD WAGNER
1813–1883

Con moto moderato

BRIDAL CHORUS

from *Lohengrin*

RICHARD WAGNER
1813–1883

Con moto moderato

ST ANTHONY CHORALE

from *Variations on a Theme by Haydn,* Op. 56a

Arranged by Rollin Smith

JOHANNES BRAHMS
1833–1897

WEDDING MARCH

from *A Midsummer Night's Dream*

Arranged by Edwin Arthur Kraft

FELIX MENDELSSOHN
1809–1847

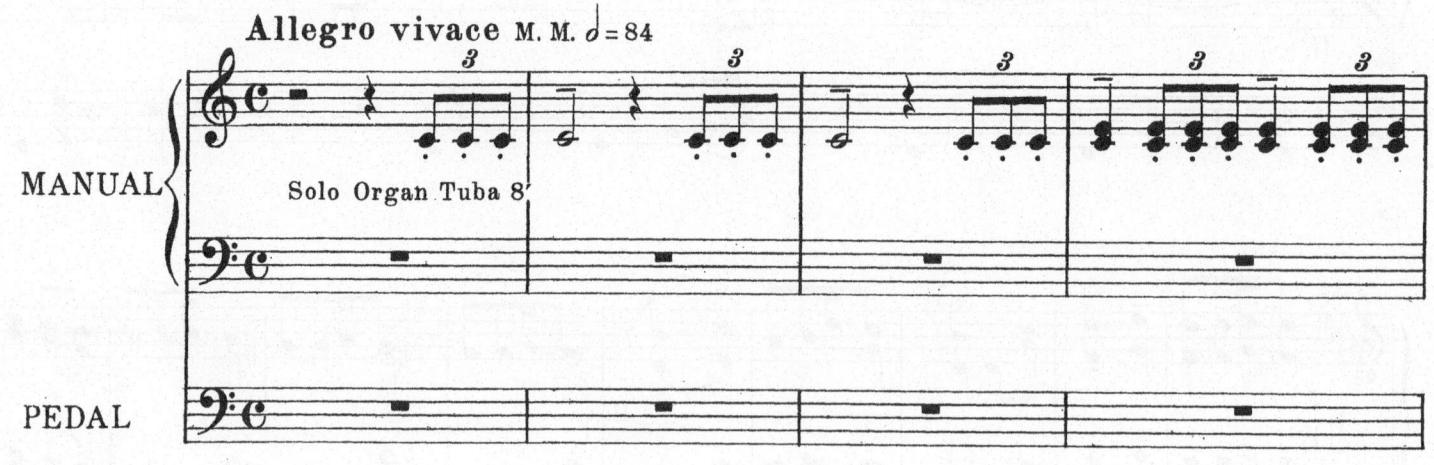

Solo Tuba

WEDDING MARCH

from *A Midsummer Night's Dream*

FELIX MENDELSSOHN
1809–1847

Allegro vivace

TUBA TUNE

Swell Flutes 16' 8' 4' 2', box open, uncoupled
Great Diapasons 16' 8' 4'
Choir or Solo Tuba
Pedal Open Wood 16' 8', Great to Pedal

NORMAN COCKER
1889–1953

BRIDAL MARCH

from *The Birds of Aristophanes*

Arranged by Walter G. Alcock

C. HUBERT H. PARRY
1848–1918

PROCESSIONAL MARCH

LEOPOLD STOKOWSKI
1882–1977

MARCHE NUPTIALE

from *Contes d'Avril*

Récit Gambes de 8, anches de 8 et de 16 préparées
Positif Fonds de 8
Grand-Orgue Flûte de 8
Pédale Basses de 8 et de 16

Arranged by the Composer

CHARLES-MARIE WIDOR
1844–1937

VOCAL MUSIC

Jesu, Joy Of Man's Desiring

Wohl mir, daß ich Jesum habe

Martin Jahn
Translated by Robert Bridges

JOHANN SEBASTIAN BACH
1685–1750

wis - dom, Love__ most__ bright,
un - cre - a - ted__ light.

Word of God, our flesh__ that fash - ion'd

With the fire of life__ im -

My Heart Ever Faithful

Mein gläubiges Herze

JOHANN SEBASTIAN BACH
1685–1750

Ave Maria

Op. 52, No. 6

Sir Walter Scott
English adaptation of Adam Stork's German
translation by Dr. Theodore Baker

FRANZ SCHUBERT
1797–1828

Ave Maria

Meditation on Bach's First Prelude

CHARLES GOUNOD
1818–1893

Panis Angelicus

CÉSAR FRANCK
1822–1890

I Love Thee

Ich liebe dich

EDVARD GRIEG
1843–1907

Light of my life whose i - mage my heart hold - eth!

Thou at whose feet I wor - ship and ad - ore!

With wings of love my spi - rit thee en -

Because

Edward Teschemacher

GUY D'HARDELOT
1858–1936

Poco Adagio

Be - cause___ you come to me___ with naught save
Lors - que j'en-tends ton pas,___ comme en un

love,___ And hold my hand and lift mine eyes a - bove,___ A
rê - ve Le fol es-poir de te re - voir s'é-lè - ve, Et

I Love You Truly

CARRIE JACOBS BOND
1862–1946

O Promise Me

REGINALD DE KOVEN
1859–1920

we can be a - lone and faith re - new,
let me sit be - side you, in your eyes

And find the hol - lows where those flow - ers
See - ing the vis - ion of our

grew,
par - a - dise

Those first sweet vi - o - lets of ear - ly spring, Which
Hear - ing God's mes - sage while the or - gan rolls Its

come in whis - pers, thrill us both, and sing Of love un - speak - a - ble that
might - y mu - sic to our ver - y souls, No Love less per - fect than a

WEDDING HYMNS

O Perfect Love

SANDRINGHAM

DOROTHY F. GURNEY

JOSEPH BARNBY
1838–1896

1. O per - fect Love, all hu - man thought trans - cend - ing,
2. O per - fect Life, be thou their full as - sur - ance
3. Grant them the joy which bright - ens earth - ly sor - row;

Low - ly we kneel in pray'r be - fore Thy throne,
Of ten - der cha - ri - ty and stead - fast faith,
Grant them the peace which calms all earth - ly strife,

That theirs may be the love that knows no end - ing,
Of pa - tient hope, and qui - et, brave en - dur - ance,
And to life's day the glor - ious un - known mor - row

Whom Thou for ev - er - more dost join in one.
With child - like trust that fears nor pain nor death.
That dawns up - on e - ter - nal love and life.

By Vows of Love Together Bound

St. James

ELEAZOR T. FITCH

RAPHAEL COURTEVILLE
1687–1735

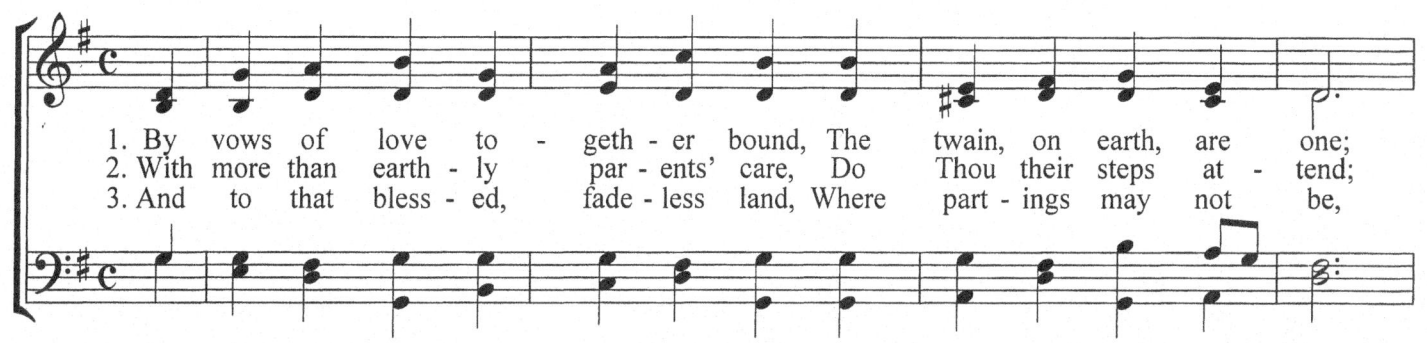

1. By vows of love to - geth - er bound, The twain, on earth, are one;
2. With more than earth - ly par - ents' care, Do Thou their steps at - tend;
3. And to that bless - ed, fade - less land, Where part - ings may not be,

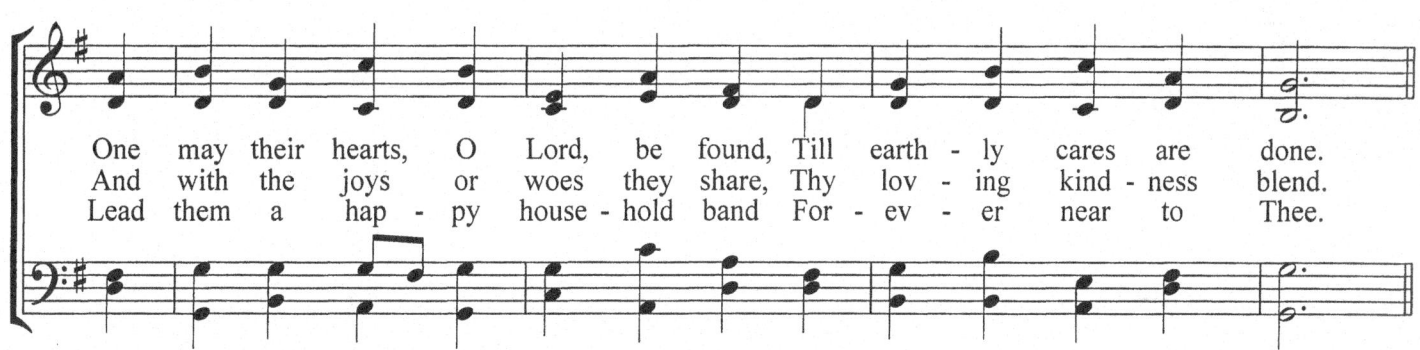

One may their hearts, O Lord, be found, Till earth - ly cares are done.
And with the joys or woes they share, Thy lov - ing kind - ness blend.
Lead them a hap - py house - hold band For - ev - er near to Thee.

As from the home of ear - lier years They wand - er, hand in hand,
O let the mem - 'ry of this hour In fu - ture years come nigh

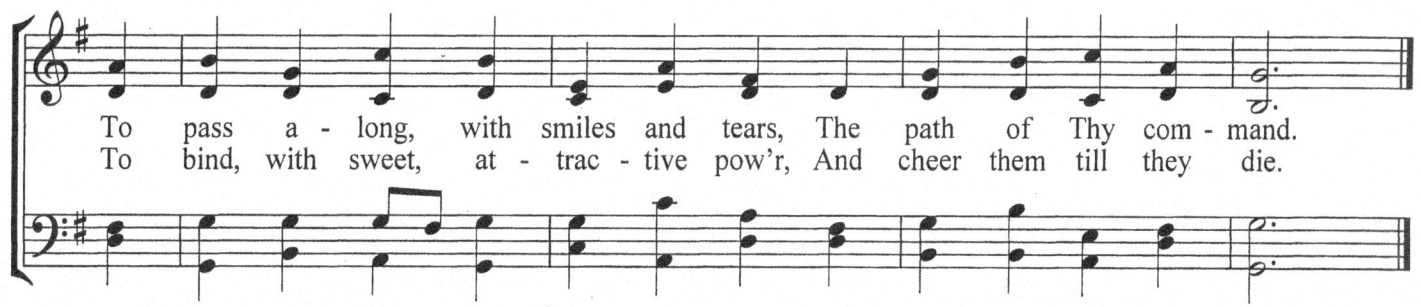

To pass a - long, with smiles and tears, The path of Thy com - mand.
To bind, with sweet, at - trac - tive pow'r, And cheer them till they die.

O Father, All Creating

GLAIRGOWRIE

John Ellerton wrote this hymn in 1876 at the request of the Duke of Westminster,
for the marriage of his daughter to the Marquis of Ormonde.

JOHN ELLERTON

JOHN BACCHUS DYKES
1823–1876

O God of Love, To Thee We Bow

ELMHURST

WILLIAM V. JENKINS

EDWIN DREWETT
dates unknown

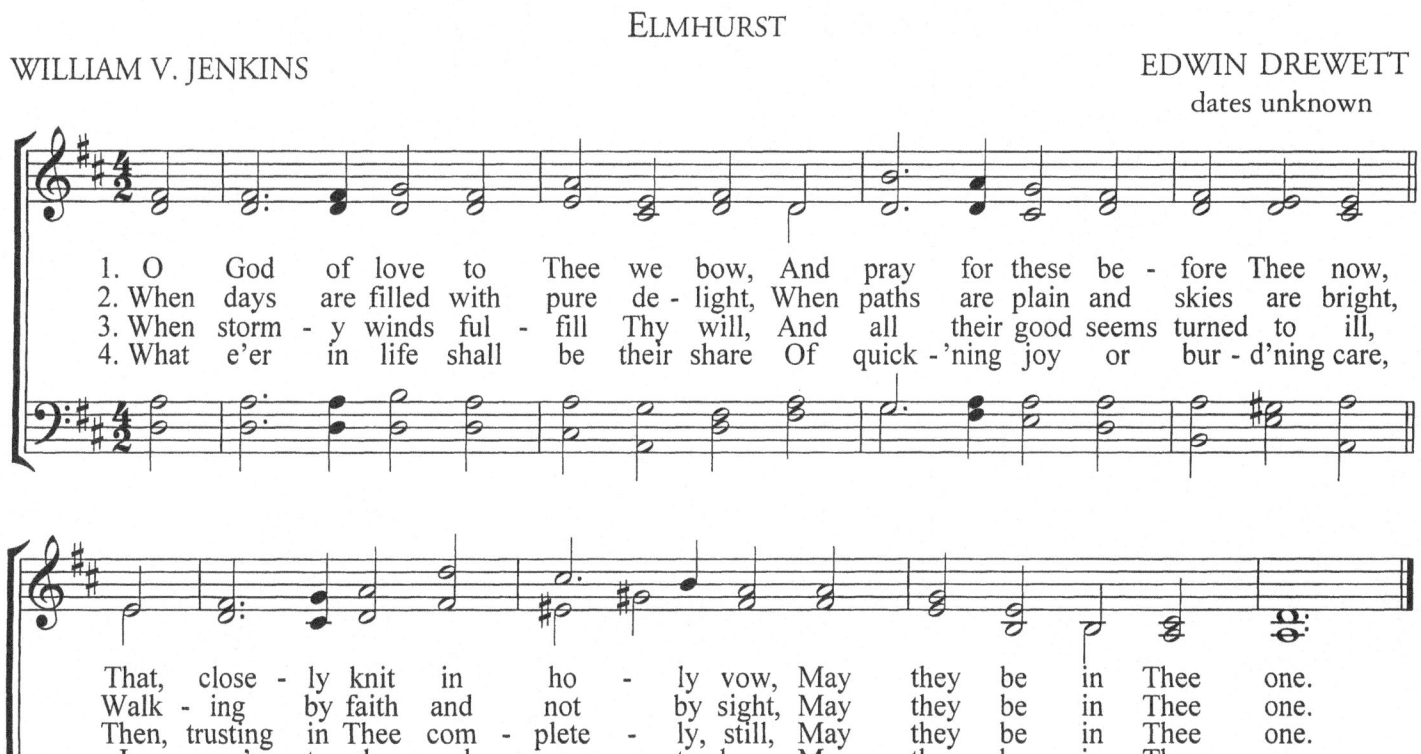

1. O God of love to Thee we bow, And pray for these be-fore Thee now,
2. When days are filled with pure de-light, When paths are plain and skies are bright,
3. When storm-y winds ful-fill Thy will, And all their good seems turned to ill,
4. What e'er in life shall be their share Of quick-'ning joy or bur-d'ning care,

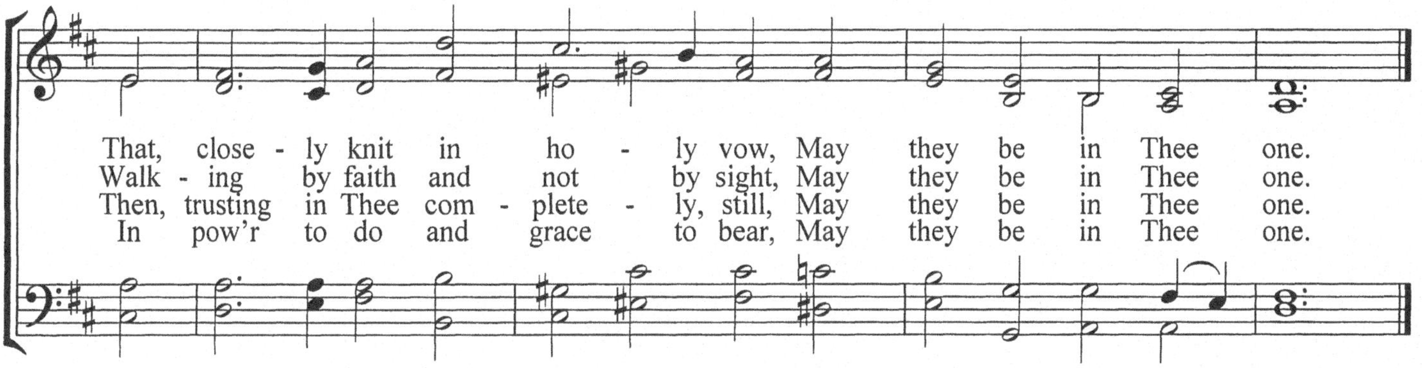

That, close-ly knit in ho-ly vow, May they be in Thee one.
Walk-ing by faith and not by sight, May they be in Thee one.
Then, trusting in Thee com-plete-ly, still, May they be in Thee one.
In pow'r to do and grace to bear, May they be in Thee one.

Since Jesus Freely Did Appear

MANOAH

JOHN BERRIDGE

GIOACCHINO ROSSINI
1792–1868

1. Since Je-sus free-ly did ap-pear To grace a mar-riage feast
2. Up-on the bri-dal pair look down, Who now have plight-ed hands;
3. With gifts of grace their heart en-dow, Of all rich dow-ries blest;
4. In pur-est love their souls u-nite, That they with Christ-ian care,

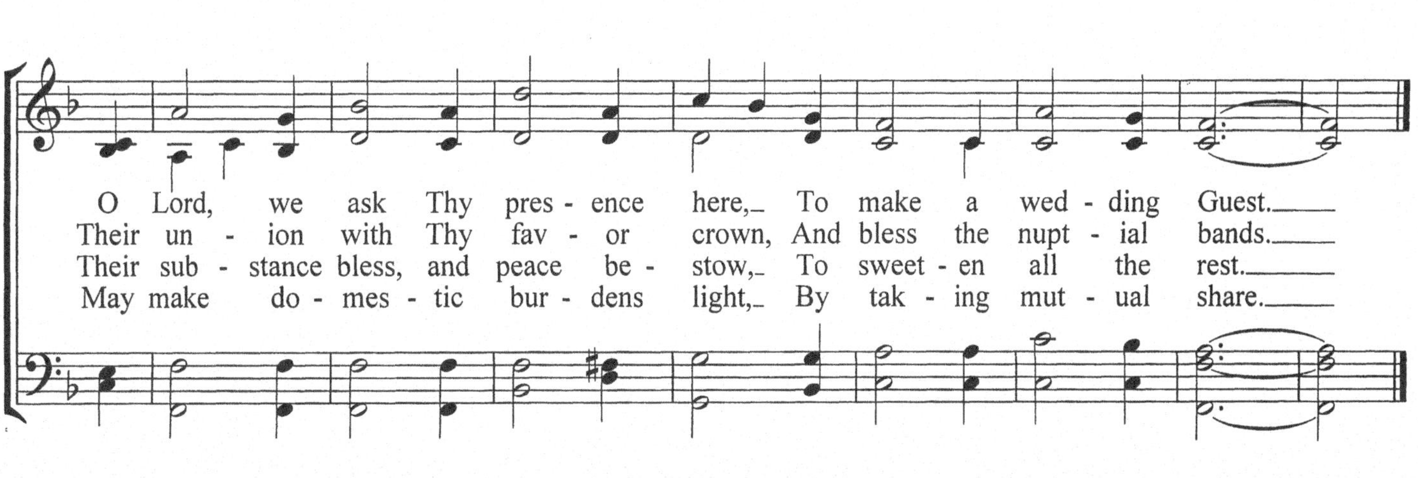

O Lord, we ask Thy pres-ence here, To make a wed-ding Guest.
Their un-ion with Thy fav-or crown, And bless the nup-tial bands.
Their sub-stance bless, and peace be-stow, To sweet-en all the rest.
May make do-mes-tic bur-dens light, By tak-ing mut-ual share.

The Voice That Breath'd O'er Eden

MAGDALENA

JOHN KEBLE

SIR JOHN STAINER
1840–1901

1. The voice that breath'd o'er E - den, That ear - liest wed - ding day,
2. Be pre - sent might - y Fa - ther, To give a - way this bride,
3. Be pres - ent, Ho - ly Spir - it, To bless them as they kneel,
4. To cast their crowns be - fore Thee In per - fect sac - ri - fice,

The pri - mal mar - riage bless - ing, It hath not passed a - way.
As thou gav'st Eve to A - dam Out of His own pierced side:
As Thou, for Christ, the Bride - groom, The heav - 'nly Spouse dost seal!
Till to the home of glad - ness With Christ's own Bride they rise.

Still in the pure e - spou - sal Of Chris - tian man and maid,
Be pres - ent, Son of Ma - ry, To join their lov - ing hands,
O spread Thy pure wing o'er them, Let no ill pow'r find place,
To Fath - er, Son, and Spir - it, The God Whom we a - dore,

The Ho - ly Three are with us, The three - fold grace is said.
As Thou didst bind two nat - ures In Thine e - ter - nal bands!
When on - ward to Thine al - tar Their hal - lowed path they trace,
Be loft - iest prais - es giv - en, Now and for ev - er - more.

O Love Divine and Golden

HOMELAND

JOHN S.B. MONSELL

SIR ARTHUR SULLIVAN
1842–1900

1. O love di - vine and gold - en, Mys - te - rious depth and height,
2. God bless these hands u - nit - ed; God bless these hearts made one!

To Thee the world be - hold - en, Looks up for life and light;
Un - sev - ered and un - blight - ed May they through life go on,

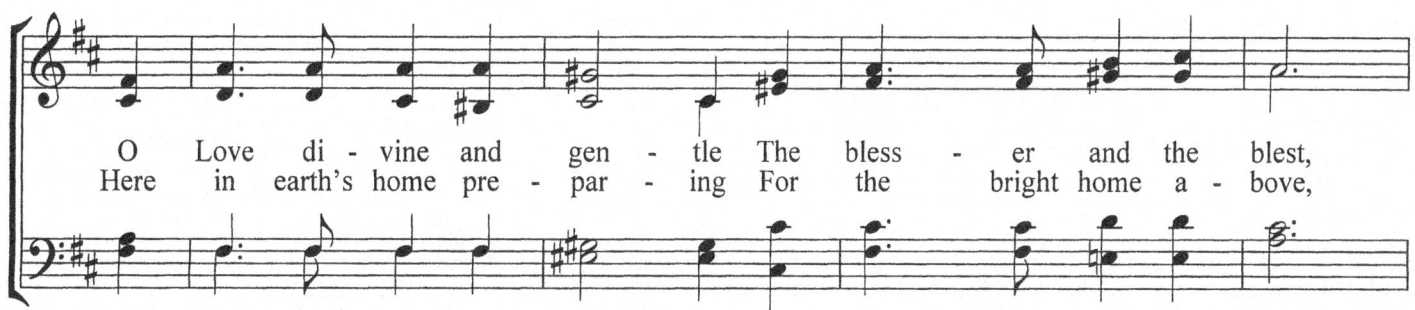

O Love di - vine and gen - tle The bless - er and the blest,
Here in earth's home pre - par - ing For the bright home a - bove,

Be - neath Thy care pa - ren - tal The world lies down in rest.
And there for - ev - er___ shar - iong Its joy where "God is Love."

Lord, Who At Cana's Wedding Feast

ST. URSULA

ADELAIDE THRUPP

FREDERICK WESTLAKE
1840–1898

1. Lord, Who at Ca - na's wed - ding feast Didst as a guest ap - pear,
2. The ho - liest vow that man can make, The gold - en thread in life,
3. On those who at Thine al - tar kneel, O Lord, Thy bless - ing pour,

Thou dear - er far than earth - ly guest Vouch - safe Thy pres - ence here;
The bond that none may dare to break, That bind - eth man and wife;
That each may wake the oth - er's zeal To love Thee more and more:

For ho - ly Thou in - deed dost prove The mar - riage vow to be,
Which, blest by Thee, what - e'er be - tides, No e - vil shall de - stroy,
O, grant them here in peace to live, In pu - ri - ty and love,

Pro - claim - ing it a type of love Be - tween the Church and Thee.
Through care - worn days each care di - vides, And dou - bles ev - 'ry joy.
And, this world leav - ing, to re - ceive A crown of life a - bove!